Love & Loss

Usha Sridhar

BookLeaf
Publishing

India | USA | UK

Presentation by *BookLeaf Publishing*

Web: www.bookleafpub.com

E-mail: info@bookleafpub.com

ISBN: 9789358314953

First edition 2023

DEDICATION

Dedicated to my Angel, my daughter who has taught me to live a life of joy and to do whatever makes me happy. This book is also dedicated to all the wonderful women and mothers without whom the world would not exist.

ACKNOWLEDGEMENT

I greatly acknowledge and Thank my husband for the wonderful support and love for me and my daughter.

Untrained…..

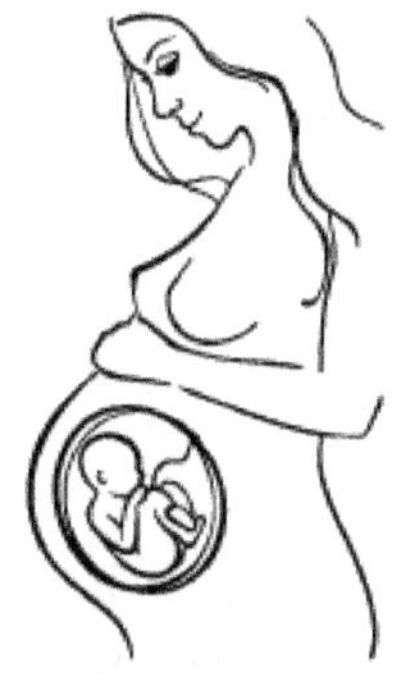

You were so little my child!
I got promoted
To being a Mother
You didn't know my Joy!
I was not trained to be a mother
I loved you though!

I learnt small things
To do for you my little child
To change diapers!
To feed you slowly!
All on the job
Just as any mother would say
I was not trained to be a mother!
I just love you!!

I learnt little things
To know when you were thirsty
To know when you were hungry
I was confused
Just as any mother would say
I was not trained to be a mother!
I just love you!!

I learnt some things
To understand your unsaid thoughts
To make you feel comfortable
At times when you heard words that hurt
Either from me or others
Little did I know what made you sad
Just as any mother would say
I was not trained to be a mother!
I just love you!!

I learnt a few more things
As you grew
That friends matter more
Later I did realize
I was the same too!
Just as any mother would say
I was not trained to be a mother!
I just love you!!

I really thought I had learnt
To be a mother
When you chose your partner
I learnt to be quiet
When you wanted time
With your newfound joy
Now I felt that I was "learned"
Just as any mother would say
I was not trained to be a mother!
I just love you!!
Now the truth is
Whether I'm trained or not
I'm your mother
No matter what
My shoulder is always available
To share your happiness
To drop any sadness
I think I'm trained
Just as any mother would say
I was not trained to be a mother!
"I just love you ....
Always and forever"

"…..Mother"

Know the Now

It's Now they say
That Now is what we have!

The Past and the Future
Are but Imaginations
Never to repeat
Never to Come
It's all just Illusions!!

It's Now they say
That Now is what we have!!

To see the clock
And plan the days
Ahead of Now
Is just a theory!!
Not worth a Dime
It's the Now
That's the Prime!

It's Now they say
That Now is what we have!!

When the Now is gone
It's again another New!
Life is too short
To quote the past
Or Plan a date
That will never last!!

It's Now they say
That Now is what we have!!

The Joy of Now
Brings us closer to life
Each to Cherish
But sure to perish!!

It's Now they say
That Now is what we have!!

Let's know the Now
The Now that's here
That None can deny!

It's Now they say
That Now is what we have!!

The Divine

In the silence of the night ...
In the chirping sound of birds at dawn....
In the sunlight that peeps through the window....
In the blade of grass with a dew drop....
In the shadow of myself .....
In the twilight of sunset....
In the buzzing sound of insects.....
And back in the silence of the night....
I see you, The Divine!
The pure and the only one!

Blessed I am

How blessed I am
To have that navel bond
That's so special
You're the only one I have!

You are the energy in me
The joy in me!
Each word you say
Each moment with you
Gives me the bliss
That you may not know.

Where are you my Angel?
Tell me now...
I've no wings to fly,
But I'll run

To catch the wings of a flight
To see you wherever you are
To be with you!

You know me more
Than I know myself
It's hard for me
To not speak to you
To not see you
So it's time
For you to be with me
Before the longing ache
Breaks me down
Into pieces a million
That you can't put back
When you see me
Later than now!

Calamities

An earthquake
A tsunami
A downpour of tears
All at the same time
How could it all come together?
But it all did ....
All at once!!

You may not feel it,
Nor see or hear it
It's the pain, the grief
That's deeper than the ocean
Higher than a tsunami
Heavier than a downpour

All of these are silently happening
The earthquake in my heart
The Tsunami in my brain
And the downpour in my eyes
Knowing not what to do
As I watch the skies
Asking the heavens to send you back!

Miss you and Love you my Angel!

Time

Time!
It seems to heal
The grief, the pain
But it really hides.

Time!
It covers the grief
With layers of smiles
It seems to heal
But it really hides.

Time!
It's a veil
So dark it is
None can see
The pain beneath
It seems to heal
But it really hides.

Time!
It flies so fast
Covering with dust
The pain beneath
When tears of grief
Pours down and clears
The pain hidden
You will know
It seems to heal
But it really hides!

Time!
A million years
May seem so long
Still not enough
To heal the sorrow
It's not a healer
It only hides!

Lost in thoughts

Lost in thoughts
No words to say
Moments go by
Like days so long
None can feel
The pain of an orphaned mother!

I can wait
Many such days
If only you tell me
When you'll be back
To make my days go by
Like moments so fast
And feel the joy
Of being with you!

Take my years!

Life is too short
I used to say and I will again
But it was for me
Not you!

I want you
To return
To take the years I've got
Since a longer life
Still awaits you!
A shorter time
For me....
To see you!

Love you and miss you - Amma.

It's still dark

It's dark everywhere
I turn on the lights
The rooms are lit
But not my soul
It's still in the dark
Without the light
That was you!

Bright were the lights
May be the wattage
But none could match
The shine of your eyes
That lit my life!
My soul lays still
In the dark
Without the light
That was you!

Unaware…

Unaware ….
We breathe
We roam
We eat
We say we know it All
We are happy!

Our ego
Our Pride
Our Jealousy
And our pretensions
What's it all?

It is the unawareness
Of our expiry date
The actual truth!
Thank God
We are unaware of this!!

Smiles outside

Smiles outside
Tears inside
With the noise of the world
Pretending to be strong
Days go by!

Nights are silent
But not the mind
For it can't pretend
And smile to itself
Lying in grief
Nights go by!

Not sure how long
The acting

The pretension
Will continue
To make the Days
And Nights go by!

The world knows not
What it feels
To drown in your own tears
Day and night
Until it's all gone by!
Love you and miss you my Angel!

Love turned Grief

That space so empty
That cannot be filled
It's a void forever
A void that turned
Love to Grief!

In that empty space
With the void you left
You made it possible
I would say
For me to know
That Love is Grief!

No light, nor water, air or dirt
Can fill this space
It's a void forever

Just filled with Grief
But I know now
That Love is Grief!

May I ask Your guidance
To lead me
Slowly and gently
Through this journey
Of Love turned Grief
To the end
Until I see you
On the other side
And turn Grief to Love again.

With love turned grief - your Amma.

The Sound of Silence

Have you heard
The sound of silence?
That lies so quiet in a soul
Listen to the silence
That can tell you tales!

'Tis the sound
That comes from the deepest of oceans
And the mountains so high
In many unreachable places
Yet so powerful
It quietly lies in a soul!

That sound, so still
Heard in deep breaths
That only you will know

Kindles the love, the peace,
The joy unbound
At times the grief, the lust,
Or the Ego to its fullest!

If only you could hear
That sound of silence
At times quieter than midnight
Often louder than a lion's roar
It is that
That brings You back
To the world of calmness
Through the pure
Sound of silence!

My little child

My Little child
Grown up, still a baby to me
Far away you go
To find and fetch what you need.

Gone are the days
When I could see
In your eyes
Your wants that I could fulfill

The Smile on your face
Made me feel the divine grace
That will linger
Until I see you again.

Your touch and feel
Though not here
Happiness it brings
With the hope
You'll be closer soon.

Love is the space
That ties all together
Dear Child
Grown up, still a baby to me.

Twilight flower

This little flower
Bloomed in our garden
Brought joy with it
That's what we wanted!!

To nurture it fully
We did transplant it faithfully!
Moving brought more joy
For the flower now brought fragrance
Unknown to us before!

What a joy it was
That this Twilight flower
Bloomed in our Garden!

It had the fragrance
It had the Beauty
That made every face smile!

It had to spread the smile
Far and wide
To all loved friends
So it did move away
From our garden
To make more faces smile!
What a joy it was
That this Twilight flower
Bloomed in our Garden!

This little flower
Had to grow more
With another support
To give the world more joy!!

To our delight
It did find
A strong yet gentle support
To guide and show the way
To enhance the beauty -
Of a New Home!
In a New Garden!!

We let that gentle guide
Show the Twilight flower
Much more happiness
That would make
Every place a joy to be!!

What a joy it is
To share this love
Of our life
The Twilight flower
That Bloomed in our Garden!

It's been a while!

It's been a while
I heard your voice - a melody!

It's been a while
I held your hand - to guide me!

It's been a while
I danced with you - a bliss it was!

It's been a while
I spoke with you - the resilience I saw!

Oh! I just realized
It's been a while
You've been gone
Never to return
To a place I can't come now!

It will be a while
But I'll see you soon.

Rainbow

I look at the sky
To see if you are shining
And smile at me through the sunrays!

I look at the clouds
To see if you are floating
And fall on me as raindrops!

I look again
To see that you've gone
As a bright ray
Into a raindrop
Turning into colors
A rainbow you are!
A love, a joy
For All!

Life goes on

No words to say
The heartache is here to stay
Life goes on
Somehow without you!

Fake smiles
Grief inside
Each foot seems a mile
Life goes on
Somehow without you!

Every step
Every thought
Brings memories
That'll never fade
Life goes on
Somehow without you!

Your soul is my life
That's how I feel
And that's real!
But Life goes on
Somehow without you!

Days are gloomy
And none can wake up
The soul in me!
For the sun in my life
Has set forever
But Life has to go on
Somehow without you!

Seventy-Eight

She was told
What She should do
What She should wear
What to Study
Whom to Marry
That She should Cook
And Clean and toil
And to rarely speak
To the end of Life!

No matter what
She's got to do it All....
Until she's about to Fall!
Chores don't bother her
Really?
Then what does?
It's the Time

It's the Energy
That's no longer there
After all the long hours!
She just turned seventy-eight!

Time has gone
She's left alone
She sees if she can
Pursue her hobbies
And her dreams
But it's just a little late
She just turned seventy-eight!

Age is but a number
But for the long hours
That went by
Pushing her dreams
A Little further each day
Until this day when....
It's just a little late
She just turned seventy-eight!

Let her heart
Be more selfish
To do
What she wants
Wear what she likes
Not to cook and clean
And toil till

The end of her lifespan
Though she is not yet
Seventy-Eight!

****

This poem is dedicated to all women.
****